The ID16™© Personality Types series

Also by Jaroslaw Jankowski

Who Are You?
The ID16™© Personality Test

Which of the sixteen personality types is yours? Are you an energetic and decisive 'administrator'? A sensitive and creative 'artist'? Or a dazzling and analytical 'logician', perhaps?

Who Are You? offers you the ID16™© Personality Test, along with an outline of the sixteen personality types, including essential information on their natural inclinations, potential strengths and weaknesses, related types, and an overview of how often each type occurs in the world population. Armed with what you discover, you'll understand yourself and others far better!

Why Are We So Different?
Your Guide to the 16 Personality Types

Why are we so very different from one another? Why do we organise our lives in such disparate ways? Why are our modes of assimilating information so varied? Why are our approaches to decision-making so diverse? Why are our forms of relaxing and 'recharging our batteries' so dissimilar?

Your Guide to the 16 Personality Types will help you to understand both yourselves and other people better. It will aid you not only in avoiding any number of traps, but also in making the most of your personal potential, as well as in taking the right decisions about your education and career and in building healthy relationships with others.

The book contains the ID16™© Personality Test, which will enable you to determine your own personality type. It also offers a comprehensive description of each of the sixteen types.

The Logician

Your Guide
to the INTP Personality Type

The Logician

Your Guide
to the INTP Personality Type

The ID16™© Personality Types series

JAROSLAW JANKOWSKI
M.Ed., EMBA

This is a book which can help you exploit your potential more fully, build healthy relationships with other people and make the right decisions about your education and career. However, it should not be considered to be a substitute for expert physiological or psychiatric consultation. Neither the author nor the publisher accept any responsibility whatsoever for any detrimental effects which may result from the inappropriate use of this book.

ID16™© is an independent typology developed by Polish educator and manager Jaroslaw Jankowski and grounded in Carl Gustav Jung's theory. It should not be confused with the personality typologies and tests proposed by other authors or offered by other institutions.

Original title: Twój typ osobowości: Logik (INTP)
Translated from the Polish by Caryl Swift
Proof reading: Lacrosse | experts in translation
Layout editing by Zbigniew Szalbot
Cover photographs by Shutterstock

Published by LOGOS MEDIA

Paperback: ISBN 978-83-7981-078-9
EPUB: ISBN 978-83-7981-079-6
MOBI: ISBN 978-83-7981-080-2

Contents

Preface

The work in your hands is a compendium of knowledge on the *logician*. It forms part of the *ID16™© Personality Types* series, which consists of sixteen books on the individual personality types and *Who Are You? The ID16™© Personality Test*, an introduction to the ID16™© independent personality typology, which is based on the theory developed by Carl Gustav Jung.

As you explore this book on the *logician*, you will find the answer to a number of crucial questions:

- How do *logicians* think and what do they feel? How do they make decisions? How do they solve problems? What makes them anxious? What do they fear? What irritates them?
- Which personality types are they happy to encounter on their road through life and which ones do they avoid? What kind of friends, life partners and parents do they make? How do others perceive them?

- What are their vocational predispositions? What sort of work environment allows them to function most effectively? Which careers best suit their personality type?
- What are their strengths and what do they need to work on? How can they make the most of their potential and avoid pitfalls?
- Which famous people correspond to the *logician*'s profile?

The book also contains the most essential information about the ID16™© typology.

We sincerely hope that it will help you in coming to know yourself and others better.

ID16™© and Jungian Personality Typology

ID16™© numbers among what are referred to as Jungian personality typologies, which draw on the theories developed by Carl Gustav Jung (1875-19161), a Swiss psychiatrist and psychologist and a pioneer of the 'depth psychology' approach.

On the basis of many years of research and observation, Jung came to the conclusion that the differences in people's attitudes and preferences are far from random. He developed a concept which is highly familiar to us today: the division of people into extroverts and introverts. In addition, he distinguished four personality functions, which form two opposing pairs: sensing-intuition and thinking-feeling. He also established that one function is dominant in each pair. He became convinced that each and every person's dominant functions are fixed and independent of external conditions and that, together, what they form is a personality type.

In 1938, two American psychiatrists, Horace Gray and Joseph Wheelwright, created the first personality test based on Jung's theories. It was designed to make it possible to determine the dominant functions within the three dimensions described by Jung, namely, **extraversion-introversion**, **sensing-intuition** and **thinking-feeling**. That first test became the inspiration for other researchers. In 1942, again in America, Isabel Briggs Myers and Katherine Briggs began using their own personality test, broadening Gray's and Wheelwright's classic, three-dimensional model to include a fourth: **judging-perceiving**. The majority of subsequent personality typologies and tests drawing on Jung's theories also take that fourth dimension into account. They include the American typology published by David W. Keirsey in 1978 and the personality test developed in the nineteen seventies by Aušra Augustinavičiūtė, a Lithuanian psychologist. Over the following decades, other European researchers followed in their footsteps, creating more four-dimensional personality typologies and tests for use in personal coaching and career counselling.

ID16™© figures among that group. An independent typology developed by Polish educator and manager Jaroslaw Jankowski, it was published in the first decade of the twenty-first century. ID16™© is based on Carl Jung's classic theory and, like other contemporary Jungian typologies, it follows a four-dimensional path, terming those dimensions the **four natural inclinations**. These inclinations are dichotomous in nature and the picture they provide gives us information regarding a person's personality type. Analysis of the first inclination is intended to determine the dominant **source of life energy**, this being either the exterior or the interior world. Analysis of the second inclination defines the dominant **mode of assimilating information**, which occurs via the senses or via intuition. Analysis of the third inclination supplies a description of the **decision-making mode**, where either mind or heart is dominant, while analysis of the fourth inclination produces a definition of the dominant **lifestyle** as either organised or spontaneous. The combination of all these natural inclinations results in **sixteen possible personality types**.

One remarkable feature of the ID16™© typology is its practical dimension. It describes the individual personality types in action – at work, in daily life and in interpersonal relations. It neither concentrates on the internal dynamics of personality nor does it undertake any theoretical attempts at explaining or commenting on invisible, interior processes. The focus is turned more toward the ways in which a given personality type manifests itself externally and how it affects the surrounding world. This emphasis on the social aspect of personality places ID16™© somewhat closer to the previously mentioned typology developed by Aušra Augustinavičiūtė.

Each of the ID16™© personality types is the result of a given person's natural inclinations. There is nothing evaluative or judgemental about ascribing a person to a given type, though. No particular personality type is 'better' or 'worse' than any other. Each type is quite simply different and each has its own potential strengths and weaknesses. ID16™© makes it possible to identify and describe those differences. It helps us to understand ourselves and discover our place in the world.

Familiarity with our personality profile enables us to make full use of our potential and work on the areas which might cause us trouble. It is an invaluable aid in everyday life, in solving problems, in building healthy relationships with other people and in making decisions relating to our education and careers.

Determining personality is a process which is neither arbitrary nor mechanical in nature. As the 'owner and user' of our personality, each and every one of us is fully capable of defining which type we belong to. The individual's role is thus pivotal. This self-identification can be achieved either by analysing the descriptions of the ID16™© personality types and steadily narrowing down the fields of choice or by taking the short cut provided by the ID16™© Personality Test.[1] The role played by each 'personality user' is equally crucial when it comes to the test, given that the outcome depends entirely on the answers they provide.

Identifying personality types helps us to know both ourselves and others. Nonetheless, it should not be treated as some kind of future-determining oracle. No personality type can ever justify our weaknesses or poor interpersonal relationships. It might, however, help us to understand their causes!

ID16™© treats personality type not as a static, genetic, pre-determined condition, but as a product of innate and acquired characteristics. As such, it is a concept which neither diminishes free will nor engages in pigeonholing people. What it does is open up new perspectives for us, encouraging us to work on ourselves and indicating the areas where that work is most needed.

---

[1] The test can be found in *Why Are We So Different? Your Guide to the 16 Personality Types* by Jaroslaw Jankowski.

The Logician (INTP)

THE ID16™© PERSONALITY TYPOLOGY

The Personality in a Nutshell

Life motto: Above all else, seek to discover the truths about the world.

In brief, *logicians* ...

are original, resourceful and creative. With a love for solving problems of a theoretical nature, they are analytical, quick-witted, enthusiastically disposed towards new concepts and have the ability to connect individual phenomena, educing general rules and theories from them. Logical, exact and inquiring, they are quick to spot incoherence and inconsistency.

Logicians are independent, sceptical of existing solutions and authorities, tolerant and open to new challenges. When immersed in thought, they will sometimes lose touch with the outside world.

The *logician's* four natural inclinations:

- source of life energy: the interior world
- mode of assimilating information: intuition
- decision-making mode: the mind
- lifestyle: spontaneous

Similar personality types:

- the Strategist
- the Innovator
- the Director

Statistical data:

- *logicians* constitute between two and three per cent of the global community;
- men predominate among *logicians* (80 per cent)
- India is an example of a nation corresponding to the *logician's* profile[2]

The Four-Letter Code

In terms of Jungian personality typology, the universal four-letter code for the *logician* is INTP.

General character traits

Logicians are extraordinarily creative, unconventional and original people. Capable of connecting disparate facts and experiences and of building comprehensive and cohesive systems from them, they are unswerving in their quest for truth and exploration of the principles and rules governing the world.

---

[2] What this means is not that all the residents of India fall within this personality type, but that Indian society as a whole possesses a great many of the character traits typical of the *logician.*

Their lives are played out primarily within their unusually rich interior world. Often minimalist in their outward lives, they strive to simplify their existence and dislike owning too many things or having a plethora of obligations. Their needs are few; they have no fondness for flamboyance and their lifestyle is plain in the extreme, an attitude which allows them to focus to the full on the problems absorbing their thoughts.

Thinking

Logicians are characterised by their extremely high level of intellectual independence. They will frequently question orthodox views, challenge existing solutions and seek for inaccuracies, imprecisions and gaps in accepted theories. Mistrustful of recognised authorities in a given field, they are strongly attached to their own opinions. Nonetheless, they are capable of verifying their previous ideas in the light of new data and perceptions. Their minds are constantly engaged in a brainstorming process which is entirely their own, with their thoughts spinning non-stop in overdrive.

Studying

Logicians enjoy both solving problems of a logical kind and helping others to understand the principles and rules governing the world and human behaviour. Learning new things and experimenting are sources of immense pleasure to them and they have the ability to systemise knowledge, forming a logical whole and endowing it with a cohesive structure. By nature, they are logicians – hence the name for this personality type – and they are also inclined to be theoreticians. As a result, they are more interested in forging theoretical concepts than putting them into practice.

They cope well with change and are generally tolerant and flexible, with the exception of situations where someone undermines their convictions or behaves in a manner which affronts their principles. When that happens, they are quite capable not only of voicing their opposition, but also of taking up the fight in defence of their arguments. Undertakings with no rational grounds underpinning them are something they approach with reservation.

Pitfalls

On the whole, *logicians* find everyday, routine activities tiresome and dislike shopping for clothes, cosmetics and toiletries, paying bills and doing the housework, viewing such chores as thieves of their valuable time. As a result, they will neglect them, be it consciously or unconsciously.

Logical discrepancies, sloppy or imprecise statements and arguments which are big on verbosity, but low on content all irritate them immensely and they have tremendous difficulty in understanding people who fail to share their fervour for seeking the truths about the world. Intellectual laziness and incompetence get their hackles up, while they are simply flabbergasted by people who have no driving urge to develop, perceiving them, for instance, as dilettantes, even when they have many years of experience working in a given area.

Academic titles, status, position and popularity make no impression on them; what they value is competence, knowledge, experience and intelligence. They enjoy the company of honest, open and genuine people, who, regardless of their field, are knowledgeable about what they do.

As others see them

Other people see *logicians* as straightforward and honest, but as people who are, nonetheless, difficult to get close to. During an initial encounter, they can give the impression of being diffident and alienated. However, amongst their friends and acquaintances, they have a greater sense of certainty, particularly when they voice their own views or theories. They can gain a reputation for being unreliable, absent-minded and none too well organised on account of the fact that, when they are excited by new ideas, they will often forget prior arrangements and promises. In general, others find their mind-set difficult to understand and, to some people, they come across as both 'too clever by half' and unduly critical, while others are irritated by their tendency to split hairs and incessantly correct everyone and everything.

Seeing and solving problems

Logicians are nimble-minded, exceptionally quick-witted people who are completely at home in the world of abstract theories and enjoy occasional surges of inspiration and illumination. They love fresh challenges, are always happy to learn something new and their attitude towards hitherto unknown concepts is an enthusiastic one. The chance to experiment is more important to them than stability and a sense of security and they love innovative and unconventional approaches to problems. Endowed with an uncommon gift for identifying hypothetical possibilities and both formulating new theories and pouring cold water on old ones, they think in atypical, unconventional ways and will thus often arrive at solutions which no one else has even approached. Their thinking is global and what interests them are comprehensive, far-reaching solutions. They perceive disparate phenomena as part of a greater whole and identify the connections between them.

Logical arguments and decisions grounded in objectivity and rationality are what carry weight with them; they remain utterly unpersuaded by activities undertaken on the basis of subjective emotions and feelings. Capable of forming a precise definition of problems and focusing on the essential, they are quick to detect any and every inaccuracy and imprecision. Their pursuit of objective truth is more important to them than other people's well-being, as is treading the path of logic; hence their belief that operating on the basis of emotions, feelings, likes and dislikes is out of the question. When they have their nose to the scent in a quest, they are both dogged in the extreme and objective to a fault. They will seek solutions to problems regardless of whether it will be of any benefit to themselves and never give up on their search, even when they can see that a potential discovery will cost them dearly, for example, by overturning a viewpoint they have held thus far.

Communication

Logicians express themselves succinctly, precisely and as faultlessly as they possibly can. Indeed, when it comes to describing reality and defining problems, their exactitude outstrips that of all the other fifteen personality types. However, they are not in the least talkative by nature and mainly speak when they have something important to say. They tend to communicate rarely and are even capable of going for lengthy periods without uttering so much as a word. They are neither numbered among those people who talk simply to kill time or keep the atmosphere friendly, nor do they set much store by convention, politeness and courteous gestures. Celebratory parties and social gatherings are torture to them.

All of this means that, at times, they may well commit various kinds of gaffes or behave tactlessly, which can be mistaken for a dislike of people. They also find it challenging to listen to pronouncements which, in their opinion, are devoid of sense or contain erroneous information. In situations of that kind, they have a tendency to put people right, a habit which can sometimes cause tension in their relationships with others and lead to their being taken as someone who 'always knows best'.

In discussions they are invincible, since matching their logical and cohesive arguments is no simple matter. They are happiest when talking about problems of a theoretical nature which are currently bothering them. However, they may not always find themselves in the company of people who share their love of that type of searching conversation.

At times, they cut themselves off from others, avoiding all contact with them. Some people may erroneously assume them to be making a show of their distance and superiority, when what they are actually doing is fulfilling their natural need for the silence and solitariness that are essential to them if they are to collect their thoughts and 'recharge their batteries'.

In the face of stress

Logicians frequently become genuine experts in the fields they are involved in. Although they are normally self-assured and conscious of their own abilities, they are also well aware of their limitations, deficiencies and defects. Indeed, there are times when they quite simply feel overwhelmed by what they feel to be the sheer magnitude of their ignorance or are tormented by their fear of failing and of making mistakes.

In stressful situations, they lose their self-assurance and either begin to react to stimuli in ways which are out of all proportion or become exceptionally suspicious and mistrustful. They love spending their free time at home. Copious readers, they also enjoy logic games. Nonetheless, even when they are 'off-duty', their minds are always intensively at work, turning the problems which are currently engaging them over in their thoughts as they continue their unending search for truths and solutions.

Socially

The interior world of *logicians* is an intensely rich one, but they often give the impression of being removed from the world around them. Neither extending their group of friends and acquaintances nor developing their relationships with other people are among their priorities and, by the same token, others find it difficult to get to know them and penetrate their world.

Logicians dislike calling attention to themselves and feel uncomfortable when they find themselves at the centre of attention. They build new acquaintanceships slowly and cautiously, being reluctant to confide in others and rarely turning to them for help, since they have a fear of becoming dependent and losing their autonomy. Accepting criticism well themselves, they are also capable of voicing critical opinions addressed to others. Nonetheless, they do their best to avoid conflict, though not at any price.

As a rule, they have difficulty both in reading other people's emotions and feelings and in expressing their own. They are better able to convey their affections and show tenderness in writing than face to face. All of this, combined with their natural scepticism, critical assessment, mistrust and tendency to set people right means that they find building relationships with others a challenging affair. They are lost in situations which call for the expression of feelings or public displays of affection and find themselves on equally shaky ground in the face of tension and conflict. In such situations, failing to grasp the importance of people's injured emotions and hurt feelings, they will try appealing to logic in an effort to analyse the situation and establish the rational causes of the problem.

Amongst friends

Logicians are happy amongst those who share their interests or are experts in a particular field. They also enjoy being with people they view as authorities and with whom they can share their reflections. As they see it, relationships with other people should serve some purpose, such as the acquisition of knowledge or a search for truths about the world, for instance. Being uncertain of themselves in the area of emotions and feelings, they endeavour to use logic as their guide in their interpersonal communications, an approach which severely limits their field of view and means that they may sometimes hurt others by their behaviour, failing to perceive that they should show someone their gratitude or appreciation of their efforts, for instance. They simply have no grasp of how this can leave people feeling disappointed or disheartened.

As a rule, they have only a few friends or close acquaintances. Those relationships, however, are extremely deep and enduring. They most often strike up friendships with *strategists*, *innovators*, *practitioners* and other *logicians* who share their enthusiasms and interests, while *advocates*, *protectors* and *presenters* will most rarely figure among their friends.

As life partners

Logicians are neither predisposed towards establishing new friendships nor interested in being popular and liked by others. Nonetheless, a solitary life in no way seems to them to be ideal. As life partners, they are extraordinarily loyal, faithful and constant in their feelings and they take their responsibilities extremely seriously. With their minimalist approach to life, their own needs are usually modest. Everyday household duties are not something they excel at and they have a tendency to forget prior arrangements, deadlines and anniversaries.

Highly tolerant by nature, they offer their partner a great deal of freedom and expect the same themselves. They bring passion and enthusiasm to their relationships via the conduit of their inventiveness, imagination and rich interior lives. At times, however, they struggle to reconcile their ideas and visions with reality. The most critical problem they face stems from their inability to identify their partner's feelings and emotional needs. They may love them dearly and yet, at one and the same time, have absolutely no grasp whatsoever of their feelings, their emotions and what they are experiencing, a character trait which is often mistakenly perceived as a lack of interest. In difficult situations and moments of crisis, they may well start seeking the rational causes underlying the problems and endeavour to solve them logically, without noticing that their partner quite simply needs them to show some care, concern, warmth and love. They are often astonished to discover that someone should expect this of them, since they themselves have no such needs. At the same time, it is an issue which can give rise to problems within their relationships.

Logicians will sometimes accuse their partner of exaggerating or making exorbitant demands. When subjected to pressure, they might well withdraw from the relationship, recognising that the situation has outgrown them and that their partner does not accept them or has expectations which are too high. Experiences of this kind mean that they will sometimes choose the single life. The natural candidates for a *logician's* life partner are people of a personality type akin to their own; *strategists*, *innovators* or *directors*. Building mutual understanding and harmonious relations will be easier in a union of that kind. Nonetheless, experience has taught us that people are also capable of creating happy and successful relationships despite what would seem to be an evident typological incompatibility. Moreover, the differences between two partners can lend added dynamics to a relationship and engender personal development. Indeed, for many people, this is a prospect that appears more attractive than the vision of a harmonious relationship wherein concord and full, mutual understanding hold sway.

As parents

As parents, *logicians* are extremely loyal to their children and have a driving urge to bring them up to be independent adults who are guided by logic and are capable of forming rational and autonomous opinions. They respect their individualism, value their opinions and allow them to take part in making decisions concerning family life. As a rule, they do not impose limitations on their offspring, but allow them a great deal of freedom and space to develop.

Their flexibility, openness and tolerance may well trigger unlooked-for side effects, since their children sometimes have problems in distinguishing good and desirable behaviour from bad and reprehensible. They also run into trouble when it comes to meeting their offspring's emotional needs and it can happen that their children will resort to radical and undesirable behaviour in an attempt to call attention to themselves. Later in life, they appreciate their *logician* parents first and foremost for teaching them to be independent and for the respect they showed for their decisions and choices.

Work and career paths

What sets *logicians'* pulses racing is working on pioneering and innovative projects and they love stepping into areas which no one else has yet explored. Characterised by both their loyalty towards their employer and the high standards of their work, they are able to evaluate other people's skills and competence in a flash. In general, they are highly demanding of themselves and of others and any manifestation whatsoever of wastefulness, perfunctoriness and laziness irritates them enormously.

Views on workplace hierarchy

Logicians appreciate knowledge, experience, intelligence and open-mindedness in their superiors and expect nothing from them barring the fact that they create a space where those they supervise can work unhindered and then refrain from interfering, leaving them alone to get on with things.

They themselves dislike leading other people, checking up on them, disciplining them and issuing them with instructions. Even so, they have a tremendous influence on others and inspire them, since they are an inexhaustible source of new ideas and have no fear of taking risks.

Enthusiasms and stumbling blocks

Logicians have no liking at all for routine activities and cope badly in positions demanding their ready availability and compliance with rigid rules and bureaucratic procedures. They approach their duties and responsibilities very seriously, but may sometimes be neglectful when it comes to formalities and official requirements such as compiling reports, for instance.

Their preference is for solving complex problems of a theoretical nature and requiring logical thought, while their enthusiasm turns more towards doing the groundwork for projects than accomplishing them. Organisational and practical aspects are something they will readily leave to others.

As part of a team

Logicians are happiest working independently. They dislike being checked up on and supervised; their need is for autonomy and independence. Indeed, at times they can be obsessive as far as their privacy is concerned. They prize peace and quiet and are most content when they can work from home. However, they are capable of organising the workloads of a group if solving a vital problem demands it.

They fit into a team relatively well when it consists not of a formal, hierarchical structure, but of a loosely connected group of enthusiastic experts committed to the matter in hand. Their liking is for a tolerant environment which offers extensive freedom of action and the space to bring creative and innovative concepts to the light of day.

Professions

Knowledge of our own personality profile and natural preferences provides us with invaluable help in choosing the optimal path in our professional careers. Experience has shown that, while *logicians* are perfectly able to work and find fulfilment in a range of fields, their personality type naturally predisposes them to the following fields and professions:

- analyst
- archaeologist
- architect
- artistic director
- chemist
- computer programmer
- computer systems expert
- detective
- economist
- expert consultant and witness
- engineer
- film producer
- financial adviser
- historian
- IT specialist
- investment and stockbroking
- lawyer
- linguist
- mathematician
- musician
- philosopher
- photographer
- research and development specialist
- risk assessment expert
- scientist
- strategy specialist
- translator
- tertiary educator
- urban and rural planning
- writer

Potential strengths and weaknesses

Like any other personality type, *logicians* have their potential strengths and weaknesses and this potential can be cultivated in a variety of ways. *Logicians'* personal happiness and professional fulfilment depend on whether they make the most of the 'pluses' offered by their personality type and face up to its inherent dangers. Here, then is a SUMMARY of those 'pluses' and dangers:

Potential strengths

Logicians are extraordinarily intelligent, creative and inventive, with the ability to connect disparate facts and experiences and build comprehensive and cohesive systems from them. Unconventional and original, their attitude towards new concepts and ideas is an enthusiastic one. Their concentration skills are extraordinary and they are impossible to distract; dragging them away from a task they deem important is a struggle, since they are more than capable of turning their entire energy towards solving whatever problem is currently engaging them. They are characterised by their high level of intellectual independence and other people's opinions make no major impression on them. If a point of view seems to them to be logically lacking in cohesion and irrational, they will discard it without regard for whether or not a recognised authority stands behind it or the majority subscribe to it.

They have the ability to make excellent use of their experiences, successes and failures alike. By nature persevering, they will usually set themselves a high benchmark and, as a result, they frequently become genuine experts in the fields they are involved in. Perfectly at home in the world of abstract theories and complex concepts, they have the gifts of assimilating them and of logical, rational thinking, along with a natural talent for mathematics and the ability to formulate their thoughts precisely and succinctly. They are quick to spot any kind of incoherence, inconsistency or logical discrepancy; at the same time, their extraordinary precision and logicality go hand in hand with their tolerance, flexibility and open-mindedness. They accord other people freedom and independence, are able to make decisions quickly and have no problem handling criticism from others.

Potential weaknesses

Logicians are extremely logical, but their logic can be subjective and selective, since they have a tendency to focus on information which is connected to their current object of interest or constitutes a confirmation of their opinions and experience. At the same time, they might well discard arguments and findings which either go against their own experience or are not grounded in logic, and they are capable of simply ignoring people who live and perceive the world in a way different from their own. They frequently involve themselves solely in things which suit their inclinations and interest them, a tendency which can eventually limit their experiences and contact with others. Indeed, it might even lead to a form of self-isolation.

Logicians find voicing their own emotions challenging. They also struggle with perceiving the emotional needs of others and may well hurt them without the slightest awareness that they have done so. Sometimes unreliable, unpunctual, forgetful and absent-minded, they cope badly with everyday, routine activities. Implementing theoretical concepts in practice is also something they have little aptitude for. In stressful situations, they are likely to react to stimuli in ways which are out of all proportion and lose their sense of self-assurance. Deprived of the possibility of engaging in what fascinates them, they may begin to construct a negatively critical attitude towards the world around them. As it develops, it becomes manifest in the form of questioning the sincere intentions of others, correcting them to an abnormal extent and criticising anything and everything which goes against their own point of view.

Personal development

Logicians' personal development depends on the extent to which they make use of their natural potential and surmount the dangers inherent in their personality type. What follows are some practical tips which, together, form a specific guide that we might call *The Logician's Ten Commandments*.

Take an interest in people

Try putting yourself in their shoes. Give some thought to what they are going through, what fascinates them, what worries them and what they fear. Ask them how they feel, what they need and what their opinions are. Show them some warmth and be more generous in your praise. Then wait and see. The difference will come as a pleasant surprise!

Learn to manage your time and set priorities

Enthusiasm is your main driving force. Nonetheless, listing priorities, establishing time frames and planning out a job are not in the least the same thing as forging chains to shackle your creativity, fetter your activities and encumber you as you carry out the task. Perish the thought! They are tools and when you use them properly they will help you achieve the goals you are aiming for.

Allow people to make mistakes

Be more restrained in your criticism and correction of others. Continually setting people right and supplementing what they say makes an appalling impression. If the matter in hand is inconsequential, let people make mistakes and go beyond the facts. No one will suffer as a result – and just think of all the energy you'll save!

Say more

Share your thoughts and ideas with others. Express your emotions. Tell people how you feel and what you are going through. You will be helping your colleagues and your nearest and dearest immensely when you do. Whatever you say, it will usually be better than remaining silent.

Broaden your horizons

Test the water with things that go beyond the world of whatever you are currently interested in. Go somewhere you have never been before, talk to people you have never got to know before, take on tasks from fields you have never been involved in before. It will give you a host of valuable ideas and mean that you start seeing the world from a wider perspective.

Stop discarding other people's ideas and opinions

Just because other people's ideas and opinions conflict with you own, this does not automatically mean that they are wrong. Before you judge them as valueless, give them some serious consideration and try to understand them. The ability to listen could well revolutionise your relationship with others.

Remember important dates and anniversaries

Arrangements to meet people, the birthdays of those closest to you and family anniversaries may seem like rather trivial matters to you in comparison to whatever it is you are involved in. They matter a great deal to other people, though. So if you are incapable of remembering them, jot them down somewhere handy – and then remember to check those notes!

Stop isolating yourself

In all likelihood, you have never enjoyed gossip, chit-chat and social get-togethers. Nonetheless, nurture your contacts with your close friends and meet up with people who like discussing the topics that interest you. You could also try getting to know people online, via discussion groups, social media or sectoral fora, for instance.

Be more practical

Give some thought to the practical aspects of your theories and ideas. To make the very most of their potential, try persuading other people to come round to them and considering ways of turning them into reality. Why leave the fruits of your work to languish, neglected and unaccomplished to the full?

Focus on the positive

Instead of concentrating on what is missing, on mistakes, logical contradictions and questioning other people's good intentions, learn to identify the positive and fix your gaze on the bright side of life.

Well-known figures

Below is a list of some well-known people who match the *logician's* profile:

- **Blaise Pascal** (1623-1662); a French mathematician, physicist, philosopher and apologist.
- **Adam Smith** (1723-1790); a Scottish moral philosopher and economist whose works include *An Inquiry into the Nature and Causes of the Wealth of Nations*.

- **James Madison** (1751-1836); the 4th president of the United States and a signatory of the American Constitution.

- **Charles Darwin** (1809-1882); an English biologist, he formulated the theory of evolution.

- **William James** (1842-1910); an American philosopher, psychologist, psychotherapist and precursor of humanistic psychology and phenomenology.

- **Carl Gustav Jung** (1875-1961); a Swiss psychiatrist and psychologist, he founded analytical psychology.

- **Albert Einstein** (1879-1955); born into a Jewish family in Germany, he was one of the greatest physicists and logicians of all time. The creator of the theory of relativity and co-creator of the wave-particle theory of light, he was awarded a Nobel Prize "for his services to Theoretical Physics, especially for his discovery of the law of the photoelectric effect".

- **Dwight David Eisenhower** (1890-1969); an American general, he became the 34th president of the United States.

- **Gregory Peck** (1916-2003); an American stage and screen actor whose filmography includes *The Guns of Navarone*.

- **George Soros** (born in 1930); an American financier, currency speculator and philanthropist of Hungarian-Jewish extraction.

- **Bob Geldof** (Robert Frederick Zenon Geldof; born in 1954); an Irish singer-songwriter and social activist.

- **J. K. Rowling** (Joanne Murray; born in 1965); an English writer, the author of the Harry Potter books.

- **Tiger Woods** (Eldrick Tont Woods; born in 1975); an American professional golfer, considered to be one of the all-time greatest representatives of the sport.

The ID16™© Personality Types in a Nutshell

The Administrator (ESTJ)

Life motto: *We'll get the job done!*

Administrators are hard-working, responsible and extremely loyal. Energetic and decisive, they value order, stability, security and clear rules. They are matter-of-fact and businesslike, logical, rational and practical and possess the capability to assimilate large amounts of detailed information.

Superb organisers, they are intolerant of ineffectuality, wastefulness and slothfulness. True to their convictions and direct in their contact with others, they present their point of view decisively and openly express critical opinions, sometimes hurting other people as a result.

The *administrator*'s four natural inclinations:

- source of life energy: the exterior world
- mode of assimilating information: via the senses
- decision-making mode: the mind
- lifestyle: organised

Similar personality types:

- the Animator
- the Inspector
- the Practitioner

Statistical data:

- *administrators* constitute between ten and thirteen per cent of the global community
- men predominate among *administrators* (60 per cent)
- the United States is an example of a nation corresponding to the *administrator's* profile[3]

Find out more!

The Administrator. Your Guide to the ESTJ Personality Type by Jaroslaw Jankowski

---

[3] What this means is not that all the residents of the USA fall within this personality type, but that American society as a whole possesses a great many of the character traits typical of the *administrator*.

The Advocate (ESFJ)

Life motto: *How can I help you?*

Advocates are well-organised, energetic and enthusiastic. Practical, responsible and conscientious, they are sincere and exceptionally gregarious.

Advocates are perceptive of human feelings, emotions and needs. They value harmony and find criticism and conflict difficult to bear. With their sensitivity to any and every manifestation of injustice, prejudice or detriment to another, they are genuinely interested in other people's problems and take real delight in helping them and tending to their needs, while often neglecting their own. They have a tendency to do everything for others and can be vulnerable to manipulation.

The *advocate*'s four natural inclinations:

- source of life energy: the exterior world
- mode of assimilating information: via the senses
- decision-making mode: the heart
- lifestyle: organised

Similar personality types:

- the Presenter
- the Protector
- the Artist

Statistical data:

- *advocates* constitute between ten and thirteen per cent of the global community
- women predominate among *advocates* (70 per cent)
- Canada is an example of a nation corresponding to the *advocate's* profile

Find out more!

The Advocate. Your Guide to the ESFJ Personality Type
by Jaroslaw Jankowski

The Animator (ESTP)

Life motto: *Let's DO something!*

Animators are energetic, active and enterprising. Fond of the company of others, they have the ability to enjoy the moment and are spontaneous, flexible and open to change.

Animators are inspirers and instigators, spurring others to act. Being logical, rational and pragmatic realists, they are wearied by abstract concepts and solutions for the future. Their focus is on solving concrete problems in the here and now. They have difficulties with organising and planning and can be impulsive, acting first and thinking later.

The *animator's* four natural inclinations:

- source of life energy: the exterior world
- mode of assimilating information: via the senses
- decision-making mode: the mind
- lifestyle: spontaneous

Similar personality types:

- the Administrator
- the Practitioner
- the Inspector

Statistical data:

- *animators* constitute between six and ten per cent of the global community
- men predominate among *animators* (60 per cent)

- Australia is an example of a nation corresponding to the *animator's* profile

Find out more!

The Animator. Your Guide to the ESTP Personality Type by Jaroslaw Jankowski

The Artist (ISFP)

Life motto: *Let's create something!*

Artists are sensitive, creative and original, with a sense of the aesthetic and natural artistic talents. Independent in character, they follow their own system of values and are optimistic in outlook, with a positive approach to life and an ability to enjoy the moment.

Helping others is a source of joy to them. They find abstract theories tedious and would rather create reality than talk about it, although starting on something new comes more easily to them than finishing what they have already started. They have difficulty in voicing their own desires and needs.

The *artist's* four natural inclinations:

- source of life energy: the interior world
- mode of assimilating information: via the senses
- decision-making mode: the heart
- lifestyle: spontaneous

Similar personality types:

- the Protector
- the Presenter
- the Advocate

Statistical data:

- *artists* constitute between six and nine per cent of the global community
- women predominate among *artists* (60 per cent)
- China is an example of a nation corresponding to the *artist's* profile

Find out more!

The Artist. Your Guide to the ISFP Personality Type
by Jaroslaw Jankowski

The Counsellor (ENFJ)

Life motto: *My friends are my world*

Counsellors are optimistic, enthusiastic and quick-witted. Courteous and tactful, they have an extraordinary gift for empathy and find joy in acting for the good of others, with no thought of themselves. They have the ability to influence other people, inspiring them, eliciting their hidden potential and giving them faith in their own powers. Radiating warmth, they draw others to them and often help them in solving their personal problems.

Counsellors can be over-trusting and have a tendency to view the world through rose-tinted glasses. With their focus on other people, they often forget about their own needs.

The *counsellor's* four natural inclinations:

- source of life energy: the exterior world
- mode of assimilating information: intuition
- decision-making mode: the heart
- lifestyle: organised

Similar personality types:

- the Enthusiast
- the Mentor
- the Idealist

Statistical data:

- *counsellors* constitute between three and five per cent of the global community
- women predominate among *counsellors* (80 per cent)
- France is an example of a nation corresponding to the *counsellor's* profile

Find out more!

The Counsellor. Your Guide to the ENFJ Personality Type by Jaroslaw Jankowski

The Director (ENTJ)

Life motto: *I'll tell you what you need to do.*

Directors are independent, active and decisive. Rational, logical and creative, when they analyse problems they look at the wider picture and are able to foresee the future consequences of human activities. They are characterised by optimism and a healthy sense of their own worth and are capable of transforming theoretical concepts into concrete, practical plans of action.

Visionaries, mentors and organisers, *directors* possess natural leadership skills. Their powerful personalities and direct and critical style can often have an intimidating effect, causing them problems in their interpersonal relationships.

The *director's* four natural inclinations:

- source of life energy: the exterior world

- mode of assimilating information: intuition
- decision-making mode: the mind
- lifestyle: organised

Similar personality types:

- the Innovator
- the Strategist
- the Logician

Statistical data:

- *directors* constitute between two and five per cent of the global community
- men predominate among *directors* (70 per cent)
- Holland is an example of a nation corresponding to the *director's* profile

Find out more!

The Director. Your Guide to the ENTJ Personality Type by Jaroslaw Jankowski

The Enthusiast (ENFP)

Life motto: *We'll manage!*

Enthusiasts are energetic, enthusiastic and optimistic. Capable of enjoying life and looking ahead to the future, they are dynamic, quick-witted and creative. They have a liking for people in general, value honest and genuine relationships and are warm, sincere and emotional. Criticism is something they handle badly. With their gift for empathy and ability to perceive people's needs, feelings and motives, they both inspire others and infect them with their own enthusiasm.

They love to be at the centre of events and are flexible and capable of improvising. Their inclination leads towards idealistic notions. Being easily distracted, they have problems with seeing things through to the end.

The *enthusiast's* four natural inclinations:

- source of life energy: the exterior world
- mode of assimilating information: intuition
- decision-making mode: the heart
- lifestyle: spontaneous

Similar personality types:

- the Counsellor
- the Idealist
- the Mentor

Statistical data:

- *enthusiasts* constitute between five and eight per cent of the global community
- women predominate among *enthusiasts* (60 per cent)
- Italy is an example of a nation corresponding to the *enthusiast's* profile

Find out more!

The Enthusiast. Your Guide to the ENFP Personality Type by Jaroslaw Jankowski

The Idealist (INFP)

Life motto: *We CAN live differently.*

Idealists are sensitive, loyal, and creative. Living in accordance with the values they hold is of immense importance to them and they both manifest an interest in the reality of the spirit and delve deeply into the mysteries of life. Wrapped up in the world's problems and open to the needs of other people, they prize harmony and balance.

Idealists are romantic; not only are they able to show love, but they also need warmth and affection themselves. With their outstanding ability to read other people's feelings and emotions, they build healthy, profound and enduring relationships. They feel that they are on very shaky ground in situations of conflict and have no real resistance to stress and criticism.

The *idealist's* four natural inclinations:

- source of life energy: the interior world
- mode of assimilating information: intuition
- decision-making mode: the heart
- lifestyle: spontaneous

Similar personality types:

- the Mentor
- the Enthusiast
- the Counsellor

Statistical data:

- *idealists* constitute between one and four per cent of the global community
- women predominate among *idealists* (60 per cent)
- Thailand is an example of a nation corresponding to the *idealist's* profile

Find out more!

The Idealist. Your Guide to the INFP Personality Type by Jaroslaw Jankowski

The Innovator (ENTP)

Life motto: *How about trying a different approach...?*

Innovators are inventive, original and independent. Optimistic, energetic and enterprising, they are people of action who love being at the centre of events and solving 'insoluble' problems. Their thoughts are turned to the future and they are curious about the world and visionary by nature. Open to new concepts and ideas, they enjoy new experiences and experiments and have the ability to identify the connections between separate events.

Innovators are spontaneous, communicative and self-assured. However, they tend to overestimate their own possibilities and have problems with seeing things through to the end. They are also inclined to be impatient and to take risks.

The *innovator's* four natural inclinations:

- source of life energy: the exterior world
- mode of assimilating information: intuition
- decision-making mode: the mind
- lifestyle: spontaneous

Similar personality types:

- the Director
- the Logician
- the Strategist

Statistical data:

- *innovators* constitute between three and five per cent of the global community
- men predominate among *innovators* (70 per cent)
- Israel is an example of a nation corresponding to the *innovator's* profile

Find out more!

The Innovator. Your Guide to the ENTP Personality Type
by Jaroslaw Jankowski

The Inspector (ISTJ)

Life motto: *Duty first.*

Inspectors are people who can always be counted on. Well-mannered, punctual, reliable, conscientious and responsible, when they give their word, they keep it. Being analytical, methodical, systematic and logical by nature, they tend be seen as serious, cold and reserved. They prize calm, stability and order, have no fondness for change and like clear principles and concrete rules.

Inspectors are hard-working, persevering and capable of seeing things through to the end. As perfectionists, they try to exercise control over everything within their sphere and are sparing in their praise. They also underrate the importance of other people's feelings and emotions.

The *inspector's* four natural inclinations:

- source of life energy: the interior world
- mode of assimilating information: via the senses
- decision-making mode: the mind
- lifestyle: organised

Similar personality types:

- the Practitioner
- the Administrator
- the Animator

Statistical data:

- *inspectors* constitute between six and ten per cent of the global community
- men predominate among *inspectors* (60 per cent)
- Switzerland is an example of a nation corresponding to the *inspector's* profile

Find out more!

The Inspector. Your Guide to the ISTJ Personality Type
by Jaroslaw Jankowski

The Logician (INTP)

Life motto: *Above all else, seek to discover the truths about the world.*

Logicians are original, resourceful and creative. With a love for solving problems of a theoretical nature, they are analytical, quick-witted, enthusiastically disposed towards new concepts and have the ability to connect individual phenomena, educing general rules and theories from them. Logical, exact and inquiring, they are quick to spot incoherence and inconsistency.

Logicians are independent, sceptical of existing solutions and authorities, tolerant and open to new challenges. When immersed in thought, they will sometimes lose touch with the outside world.

The *logician's* four natural inclinations:

- source of life energy: the interior world
- mode of assimilating information: intuition
- decision-making mode: the mind
- lifestyle: spontaneous

Similar personality types:

- the Strategist
- the Innovator
- the Director

Statistical data:

- *logicians* constitute between two and three per cent of the global community;
- men predominate among *logicians* (80 per cent)
- India is an example of a nation corresponding to the *logician's* profile

Find out more!

The Logician. Your Guide to the INTP Personality Type by Jaroslaw Jankowski

The Mentor (INFJ)

Life motto: *The world CAN be a better place!*

Mentors are creative and sensitive. With their gaze fixed firmly on the future, they spot opportunities and potential imperceptible to others. Idealists and visionaries, they are geared towards helping people and are conscientious, responsible and, at one and the same time, courteous, caring and friendly. They strive to understand the mechanisms governing the world and view problems from a wide perspective.

Superb listeners and observers, *mentors* are characterised by their extraordinary empathy, intuition and trust of people and are capable of reading the feelings and emotions of others. They find criticism and conflict difficult to bear and can come across as enigmatic.

The *mentor's* four natural inclinations:

- source of life energy: the interior world
- mode of assimilating information: intuition
- decision-making mode: the heart
- lifestyle: organised

Similar personality types:

- the Idealist
- the Counsellor
- the Enthusiast

Statistical data:

- *mentors* constitute one per cent of the global community and are the most rarely occurring of the sixteen personality types
- women predominate among *mentors* (80 per cent)
- Norway is an example of a nation corresponding to the *mentor's* profile

Find out more!

The Mentor. Your Guide to the INFJ Personality Type by Jaroslaw Jankowski

The Practitioner (ISTP)

Life motto: *Actions speak louder than words.*

Practitioners are optimistic and spontaneous, with a positive approach to life. Reserved and independent, they hold true to their personal convictions and view external principles and norms with scepticism. They find abstract concepts and solutions for the future tiresome and would far rather roll up their sleeves and get to work on solving tangible and concrete problems.

Adapting well to new places and situations, they enjoy fresh challenges and risks and are capable of keeping a cool head in the face of threats and danger. Their general reticence and extreme reserve when it comes to expressing their opinions mean that other people may often find them impenetrable.

The *practitioner's* four natural inclinations:

- source of life energy: the interior world
- mode of assimilating information: via the senses
- decision-making mode: the mind
- lifestyle: spontaneous

Similar personality types:

- the Inspector
- the Animator
- the Administrator

Statistical data:

- *practitioners* constitute between six and nine per cent of the global community
- men predominate among *practitioners* (60 per cent)
- Singapore is an example of a nation corresponding to the *practitioner's* profile

Find out more!

The Practitioner. Your Guide to the ISTP Personality Type by Jaroslaw Jankowski

The Presenter (ESFP)

Life motto: *Now is the perfect moment!*

Presenters are optimistic, energetic and outgoing, with the ability to enjoy life and have fun to the full. Practical, flexible and spontaneous at one and the same time, they enjoy change and new experiences, coping badly with solitude, stagnation and routine.

With their liking for being at the centre of attention, they are natural-born actors and their speaking abilities arouse the interest and enthusiasm of their listeners. Focused as they are on the present moment, they will sometimes lose sight of their long-term aims and can also have problems with foreseeing the consequences of their actions.

The *presenter's* four natural inclinations:

- source of life energy: the exterior world
- mode of assimilating information: via the senses
- decision-making mode: the heart
- lifestyle: spontaneous

Similar personality types:

- the Advocate
- the Artist
- the Protector

Statistical data:

- *presenters* constitute between eight and thirteen per cent of the global community
- women predominate among *presenters* (60 per cent)
- Brazil is an example of a nation corresponding to the *presenter's* profile

Find out more!

The Presenter. Your Guide to the ESFP Personality Type
by Jaroslaw Jankowski

The Protector (ISFJ)

Life motto: *Your happiness matters to me.*

Protectors are sincere, warm-hearted, unassuming, trustworthy and extraordinarily loyal. With their ability to perceive people's needs and their desire to help them, they will always put others first. Practical, well-organised and gifted with both an eye and a memory for detail, they are responsible, hard-working, patient, persevering and capable of seeing things through to the end.

Protectors set great store by tranquillity, stability and friendly relations with others and are skilled at building bridges between people. By the same token, they find conflict and criticism difficult to bear. Given their powerful sense of duty and their constant readiness to come to the aid of others, they can end up being used by people.

The *protector's* four natural inclinations:

- source of life energy: the interior world
- mode of assimilating information: via the senses
- decision-making mode: the heart
- lifestyle: organised

Similar personality types:

- the Artist
- the Advocate
- the Presenter

Statistical data:

- *protectors* constitute between eight and twelve per cent of the global population
- women predominate among *protectors* (70 per cent)
- Sweden is an example of a nation corresponding to the *protector's* profile

Find out more!

The Protector. Your Guide to the ISFJ Personality Type
by Jaroslaw Jankowski

The Strategist (INTJ)

Life motto: *I can certainly improve this.*

Strategists are independent and outstandingly individualistic, with an immense seam of inner energy. Creative, inventive and resourceful, others perceive them as competent, self-assured and, at one and the same time, distant and enigmatic. No matter what they turn their attention to, they will always look at the bigger picture and they have a driving urge to improve the world around them and set it in order.

Well-organised, responsible, critical and demanding, they are difficult to knock off balance – and just as hard to please to the full. Reading the emotions and feelings of others is something they find very problematic.

The *strategist's* four natural inclinations:

- source of life energy: the interior world
- mode of assimilating information: intuition
- decision-making mode: the mind
- lifestyle: organised

Similar personality types:

- the Logician
- the Director
- the Innovator

Statistical data:

- *strategists* constitute between one and two per cent of the global community
- men predominate among *strategists* (80 per cent)
- Finland is an example of a nation corresponding to the *strategist's* profile

Find out more!

The Strategist. Your Guide to the INTJ Personality Type by Jaroslaw Jankowski

Additional information

The four natural inclinations

1. THE DOMINANT SOURCE OF LIFE
   ENERGY

   a. THE EXTERIOR WORLD
      People who draw their energy from
      outside. They need activity and contact
      with others and find being alone for any
      length of time hard to bear.

   b. THE INTERIOR WORLD
      People who draw their energy from their
      inner world. They need quiet and solitude
      and feel drained when they spend any
      length of time in a group.

2. THE DOMINANT MODE OF ASSIMILATING INFORMATION

a. VIA THE SENSES

People who rely on the five senses and are persuaded by facts and evidence. They have a liking for methods and practices which are tried and tested and prefer concrete tasks and are realists who trust in experience.

b. VIA INTUITION

People who rely on the sixth sense and are driven by what they 'feel in their bones'. They have a liking for innovative solutions and problems of a theoretical nature and are characterised by a creative approach to their tasks and the ability to predict.

3. THE DOMINANT DECISION-MAKING MODE

a. THE MIND

People who are guided by logic and objective principles. They are critical and direct in expressing their opinions.

b. THE HEART

People who are guided by their feelings and values. They long for harmony and mutual understanding with others.

4. THE DOMINANT LIFESTYLE

a. ORGANISED

People who are conscientious and

organised. They value order and like to operate according to plan.

b.   SPONTANEOUS
People who are spontaneous and value freedom of action. They live for the moment and have no trouble finding their feet in new situations.

The approximate percentage of each personality type in the world population

Personality Type:	Proportion:
• The Administrator (ESTJ):	10-13%
• The Advocate (ESFJ):	10-13%
• The Animator (ESTP):	6-10%
• The Artist (ISFP):	6-9%
• The Counsellor (ENFJ):	3-5 %
• The Director (ENTJ):	2-5%
• The Enthusiast (ENFP):	5-8%
• The Idealist (INFP):	1-4%
• The Innovator (ENTP):	3-5%
• The Inspector (ISTJ):	6-10%
• The Logician (INTP):	2-3%
• The Mentor (INFJ):	ca. 1%
• The Practitioner (ISTP):	6-9%
• The Presenter (ESFP):	8-13%
• The Protector (ISFJ):	8-12%
• The Strategist (INTJ):	1-2%

The approximate percentage of women and men of each personality type in the world population

Personality Type:	Women / Men:
• The Administrator (ESTJ):	40% / 60%
• The Advocate (ESFJ):	70% / 30%
• The Animator (ESTP):	40% / 60%
• The Artist (ISFP):	60% / 40%
• The Counsellor (ENFJ):	80% / 20%
• The Director (ENTJ):	30% / 70%
• The Enthusiast (ENFP):	60% / 40%
• The Idealist (INFP):	60% / 40%
• The Innovator (ENTP):	30% / 70%
• The Inspector (ISTJ):	40% / 60%
• The Logician (INTP):	20% / 80%
• The Mentor (INFJ):	80% / 20%
• The Practitioner (ISTP):	40% / 60%
• The Presenter (ESFP):	60% / 40%
• The Protector (ISFJ):	70% / 30%
• The Strategist (INTJ):	20% / 80%

Recommended publications

The ID16™© Personality Types series

by Jaroslaw Jankowski

The series consists of sixteen books on the individual personality types:

- *The Administrator. Your Guide to the ESTJ Personality Type*
- *The Advocate. Your Guide to the ESFJ Personality Type*
- *The Animator. Your Guide to the ESTP Personality Type*
- *The Artist. Your Guide to the ISFP Personality Type*
- *The Counsellor. Your Guide to the ENFJ Personality Type*
- *The Director. Your Guide to the ENTJ Personality Type*
- *The Enthusiast. Your Guide to the ENFP Personality Type*
- *The Idealist. Your Guide to the INFP Personality Type*
- *The Innovator. Your Guide to the ENTP Personality Type*
- *The Inspector. Your Guide to the ISTJ Personality Type*
- *The Logician. Your Guide to the INTP Personality Type*
- *The Mentor. Your Guide to the INFJ Personality Type*

- *The Practitioner. Your Guide to the ISTP Personality Type*
- *The Presenter. Your Guide to the ESFP Personality Type*
- *The Protector. Your Guide to the ISFJ Personality Type*
- *The Strategist. Your Guide to the INTJ Personality Type*

The series offers a comprehensive description of each of the sixteen types. As you explore them, you will find the answer to a number of crucial questions:

- How do the people who fall within a particular personality type think and what do they feel? How do they make decisions? How do they solve problems? What makes them anxious? What do they fear? What irritates them?
- Which personality types are they happy to encounter on their road through life and which ones do they avoid? What kind of friends, life partners and parents do they make? How are they perceived by others?
- What are their vocational predispositions? What sort of work environments allow them to function most effectively? Which careers best suit their personality type?
- What are their strengths and what do they need to work on? How can they make the most of their potential and avoid pitfalls?
- Which famous people fall within a particular personality type?
- Which nation displays the most features characteristic of a given type?

The books also contain the most essential information about the ID16™© typology.

Who Are You?
The ID16™© Personality Test

by Jaroslaw Jankowski

Which of the sixteen personality types is yours? Are you an energetic and decisive 'administrator'? A sensitive and creative 'artist'? Or a dazzling and analytical 'logician', perhaps?

Who Are You? offers you the ID16 Personality Test, along with an outline of the sixteen personality types, including essential information on their natural inclinations, potential strengths and weaknesses, related types, and an overview of how often each type occurs in the world population. Armed with what you discover, you'll understand yourself and others far better!

Why Are We So Different?
Your Guide to the 16 Personality Types

by Jaroslaw Jankowski

Why are we so very different from one another? Why do we organise our lives in such disparate ways? Why are our modes of assimilating information so varied? Why are our approaches to decision-making so diverse? Why are our forms of relaxing and 'recharging our batteries' so dissimilar?

Your Guide to the 16 Personality Types will help you to understand both yourselves and other people better. It will aid you not only in avoiding any number of traps, but also in making the most of your personal potential, as well as in taking the right decisions about your education and career and in building healthy relationships with others.

The book contains the ID16™© Personality Test, which will enable you to determine your own personality type. It also offers a comprehensive description of each of the sixteen types.

Bibliography

- Arraj, Tyra & Arraj, James: *Tracking the Elusive Human, Volume 1: A Practical Guide to C.G. Jung's Psychological Types, W.H. Sheldon's Body and Temperament Types and Their Integration*, Inner Growth Books, 1988

- Arraj, James: *Tracking the Elusive Human, Volume 2: An Advanced Guide to the Typological Worlds of C. G. Jung, W.H. Sheldon, Their Integration, and the Biochemical Typology of the Future*, Inner Growth Books, 1990

- Berens, Linda V.; Cooper, Sue A.; Ernst, Linda K.; Martin, Charles R.; Myers, Steve; Nardi, Dario; Pearman, Roger R.; Segal, Marci; Smith, Melissa: *A Quick Guide to the 16 Personality Types in Organizations: Understanding Personality Differences in the Workplace*, Telos Publications, 2002

- Geier, John G. & Dorothy E. Downey: *Energetics of Personality*, Aristos Publishing House, 1989

- Hunsaker, Phillip L. & Anthony J. Alessandra: *The Art of Managing People*, Simon and Schuster, 1986

- Jung, Carl Gustav: *Psychological Types (The Collected Works of C. G. Jung, Vol. 6)*, Princeton University Press, 1976

- Kise, Jane A. G.; Stark, David & Krebs Hirsch, Sandra: *LifeKeys: Discover Who You Are*, Bethany House, 2005

- Kroeger, Otto & Thuesen, Janet: *Type Talk or How to Determine Your Personality Type and Change Your Life*, Delacorte Press, 1988

- Lawrence, Gordon: *People Types and Tiger Stripes*, Center for Applications of Psychological Type, 1993

- Lawrence, Gordon: *Looking at Type and Learning Styles*, Center for Applications of Psychological Type, 1997

- Maddi, Salvatore R.: *Personality Theories: A Comparative Analysis*, Waveland, 2001

- Martin, Charles R.: *Looking at Type: The Fundamentals Using Psychological Type To Understand and Appreciate Ourselves and Others*, Center for Applications of Psychological Type, 2001

- Meier C.A.: Personality: *The Individuation Process in the Light of C. G. Jung's Typology*, Daimon Verlag, 2007

- Pearman, Roger R. & Albritton, Sarah: *I'm Not Crazy, I'm Just Not You: The Real Meaning of the Sixteen Personality Types*, Davies-Black Publishing, 1997

- Segal, Marci: Creativity and Personality Type: *Tools for Understanding and Inspiring the Many Voices of Creativity*, Telos Publications, 2001

- Sharp, Daryl: Personality Type: *Jung's Model of Typology*, Inner City Books, 1987

- Spoto, Angelo: *Jung's Typology in Perspective*, Chiron Publications, 1995

- Tannen, Deborah: *You Just Don't Understand*, William Morrow and Company, 1990

- Thomas, Jay C. & Segal, Daniel L.: *Comprehensive Handbook of Personality and Psychopathology, Personality and Everyday Functioning*, Wiley, 2005

- Thomson, Lenore: *Personality Type: An Owner's Manual*, Shambhala, 1998
- Tieger, Paul D. & Barron-Tieger Barbara: *Just Your Type: Create the Relationship You've Always Wanted Using the Secrets of Personality Type*, Little, Brown and Company, 2000
- Von Franz, Marie-Louise & Hillman, James: *Lectures on Jung's Typology*, Continuum International Publishing Group, 1971

About the Author

Jaroslaw Jankowski holds a Master of Education degree from Nicolaus Copernicus University in Toruń, Poland and an MBA from the Brennan School of Business at the Dominican University in River Forest, Illinois, USA. The research and development director of an international NGO and an entrepreneur, he is also involved in voluntary work. He is not only committed to promoting knowledge about personality types, but is also the creator of ID16™©, an independent personality typology based on the theory developed by Carl Gustav Jung.

Putting the Reader first.

An Author Campaign Facilitated by ALLi.

Lightning Source UK Ltd.
Milton Keynes UK
UKHW011820030120
356331UK00001B/174/P